CW00409369

Why Wing Chun Works

Alan Gibson

SUMMERSDALE

First published 1998.
Reprinted 2000, 2002 and 2003.

This edition copyright © Alan Gibson 2002

All rights reserved. The right of Alan Gibson to be identified as the author of this work has been asserted in accordance with the Copyright, Designs and Patents Act of 1988.

No part of this book may be reproduced by any means, nor translated into a machine language, without the written permission of the publisher.

Summersdale Publishers Ltd
46 West Street
Chichester
West Sussex
PO19 1RP
United Kingdom

www.summersdale.com

www.wingchun.org.uk

Printed and bound in Great Britain.

ISBN 1 84024 214 0

Important note

If you have or believe you may have a medical condition the techniques outlined in this book should not be attempted without first consulting your doctor. Some of the techniques in this book require a high level of fitness and suppleness and should not be attempted by someone lacking such fitness. The author and the publishers cannot accept any responsibility for any proceedings or prosecutions brought or instituted against any person or body as a result of the use or misuse of any techniques described in this book or any loss, injury or damage caused thereby.

Without Whom

Simon Hayes produced the illustrations and Ben Ingoldby for the technical photography (b_ingoldby@hotmail.com). Ross Mathews for additional photography. Neil Biddlecombe for the front cover design. Andre Ibbett for help in the history section. John McFarlane for help in the philosophy section, Vix Darby for the cartoons and Phil Hull for modelling. Liz Kent, Jonny Templeton, John Brogden, and Pete Harvey also helped me overcome technical problems. Without the above people this book could never have been produced.

I would also like to thank; Master Ip Chun, Clive Potter, and Master Wan Kam Leung.

Finally I would thank all my students and everyone I have ever stuck hands with, I have learned everything from you.

Contents

Preface

"Wing Chun" is a subtle and complete system of Chinese Kung Fu. Developed over hundreds of years, its roots lie in the Shaolin Temple tradition.

Legend has it that in 1645 a Buddhist nun by the name of Ng Moi devised the system and taught it to a young girl called Yim Wing Chun, who successfully used her newly learned skills to defend herself against a local bully who attempted to force himself upon her.

Originally a very secret system, the sophisticated art of Wing Chun was only passed on to family members and close, trusted friends. It was only when the legendary Grandmaster Yip Man (now sadly passed away) arrived in Hong Kong that the style was taught more openly.

Wing Chun does not pit strength against strength but rather employs its unique understanding of angles and sensitivity to force to overcome aggression (fitness, age & gender are of little consequence). Many of the exercises are scientific in approach, and the systematic training methods can be carried out in a friendly atmosphere of co-operation as opposed to one of aggressive competition. This allows students to develop freely and at their own pace.

It is possible for a complete novice to become competent within one year, although, as with any true art, practical ability is only the beginning. There is always room for deeper exploration, further development and personal interpretation.

The effectiveness of Wing Chun as a practical self-defence or street fighting method is well documented, it has been refined over the years for economy and direct application. The style does not easily lend itself to display or sport as some more flamboyant styles do, this is because the apparent simplicity of the system disguises the devastating power and speed behind its subtle technique.

Typical techniques include; trapping hands, swift low kicks, close body control and short, fast, very accurate strikes from the hands.

Introduction

I have deliberately attempted to keep this text free from specific techniques (please see my next book). By dealing with concepts and, biomechanical principles, it is my hope that the writing will be more accessible to the diverse family of Wing Chun, and be of interest to other martial artists (many techniques can spring from a few simple concepts but not vice versa).

I have attempted to explain: how Wing Chun works, why it is so effective in practice and why its methods are so different to other arts. Wing Chun has many logical and systematic learning methods, similarly this book is divided into sections to illustrate the learning process, and to make cross referencing simple.

There are of course many different theories involved in learning Wing Chun, and many different ways to apply the system. I have described the way that I personally teach because it works for me. I have also employed the use of analogies and anecdotes to explain what Wing Chun feels like and to try to put into words what it means to me on a personal and philosophical level.

Many attempts have been made to produce "How to do it" books and videos. Often they fall at the first hurdle; claiming that you can learn the entire system from their wisdom alone. Of course it is nigh on impossible to learn Wing Chun properly without a partner. Secondly, it is difficult to improve when there is nobody to compare skills with and lastly nothing can replace a good, experienced teacher.

A good teacher?

Teaching anything, on any level, is a skill in itself requiring good communication skills and an open mind. Students should be actively encouraged to question and enquire about what they are learning. You should never do something just because you have been told to or because it's traditional. In the same way you should never be refused information because "it's a secret".

If a student asks a question it should be answered in a clear, precise (and if possible scientifically provable) manner taking into account the level of understanding of the student. It should not be garbled away under a thick veneer of mystical language and mumbo jumbo nor, as some people seem to advocate, with a punch on the nose! This kind of attitude is at its best unhelpful and at its worst, complete deception.

A teacher should be respected for their ability to teach well. You should never fear your teacher, intimidation is a tactic used by the insecure to disguise their own inadequacies. In the end what matters to a student is not the race of the teacher, not how strong or fast, nor even how skilful or highly qualified the teacher is, but how well the teacher can communicate skill to the student.

Once a student has learned a skill it is often a good idea for them to explain the theory to, or practise it with beginners. This will not only consolidate their understanding in that area but will also help to groom them to be good teachers in the future.

Many martial arts are allegedly shrouded in mystery and controversy; this is in no way beneficial to anybody wishing to learn. There are no secrets in Wing Chun, only different interpretations.

Traditional V's Modified

As with any art we learn our skill from a teacher and then, as our level progresses, personal style will begin to develop. Eventually our style may be quite different to that of our teachers. This is because we have the ability to think for ourselves. Innovation is normal, healthy and in the nature of all arts; life would be incredibly dull if there was no variety.

As long as we stay within the fundamental guidelines set down for the style there are no restrictions. People who have a difference of opinion should be able to communicate and discuss, preferably through exercises such as Chi sau [see page 97] as opposed to bickering and fighting. Fighting, whether in a cage, ring, or on the street, proves nothing other than; one individual can beat another under the set of circumstances that existed at the time and place that the fight took place. Learning Wing Chun as an art does not undermine its effectivness.

The friendly and mutual exchange of ideas between different groups (and styles) can only be beneficial to all concerned. Through this process a student can learn to deal with a wider spectrum of situations and become accustomed to the very diverse ways in which different groups use technique and energy. Of course some people will never see another person's point of view, but one is not always right and the other wrong, sometime both are correct in different ways, or on different levels of understanding.

Tradition history and legend

Much of the ancient history of Wing Chun is legend, deeply embellished for political reasons, and as such, cannot be proven. There are many different versions of its past. Much of the documentation that may have existed has been destroyed, either in the burning of the Shaolin temple, or during the Cultural Revolution. As a result of this, 'evidence' often tends to be constructed out of hearsay and cannot always be considered reliable. The movements of Yip Man during his life are well documented by his eldest son Ip Chun in the book "Grandmaster Yip Man Centenary Birth" (1993).

The Shaolin Temple

The Shaolin temples are known to have been important in the teaching of kung fu, as well as the development of secret societies such as the Triads, White Lotus, Eight Trigrams, and the Boxers. The first Shaolin temple was situated in Honan province, built around AD. 495 by Emperor Hsiao Wen of the Northern Wei dynasty.

Shaolin was very influential in spreading Buddhism in the East. The main temple is situated at the foot of the Songshan or 'Central Mountain'. The temple was originally built for an Indian monk named Batuo, or Fo Tuo as he is known to the Chinese. His statue can often be found in Chinese Buddhist monasteries: a large, friendly monk.

Later in the sixth century AD another Indian monk, Bodiharma, known as Ta Mo in Chinese, visited the Shaolin temple where he taught meditation techniques to the monks. His teachings became the foundation of a new school of Buddhism known as Ch'an in China and later Zen, in Japan. The monks had to withstand long periods of meditation, to help them overcome fatigue, Ta Mo taught them breathing techniques and exercises that are thought to have been the start of martial arts.

At its most prosperous time, about 1300 years ago, the temple housed around 1500 monks, 500 of whom were skilled in combat. The Emperor Tai Tsung asked the temple to train a small force of fighting monks that he could rely on whenever he was in danger. The grateful emperor tried to persuade these monks to be full time bodyguards at his court, but they turned him down, saying it was also their duty to protect the Shaolin temple and the monks who lived there.

Around 1000 years later another emperor asked the temple for help. In 1674, 128 monks led by a former Ming partisan Cheng Kwan-Tat, went to the aid of the Ching Emperor K'ang-Hsi. Cheng had previously fought against the Manchu Emperors and then retired to temple to study. The fighting monks were a great help to the Emperor but after the battle they too turned down the chance of working full time for the Emperor, preferring instead to return to the temple.

The Emperor was persuaded that it was an insult to be turned down in this manner, so he sent an army led by a renegade monk, Ma Ning Yee, to attack the monastery. Only a few monks survived the attack and the temple was burned to the ground. Five of the surviving monks set out to devise new and better fighting systems.

They became known as the Five Ancestors, or The Venerable Five, and are believed to be responsible for the surviving

Shaolin styles. As their original arts took many years to master, it was deemed critical that any new art could be taught in a far shorter time, as existing masters were surrendering to the Manchu government.

Mid 1600's

The monks started to develop the principles of this new art but before it could be put into practice the temple was raided again with the loss of many monks. One of the escapees was a Buddhist nun named Ng Moi she was the eldest and most proficient in boxing skills. With her acquired knowledge and with the aid of some documentation written by the murdered monks, she taught a young girl with the name Yim Wing Chun (Beautiful Spring-time), representing hope for the future. The system was later named after her and she is said to have used it to successfully repel an unwanted suitor.

1700-1800

In time, Yim Wing Chun married and shared her knowledge with her husband Leung Bok Chow who became a very proficient exponent of the art. Leung Bok Chow passed his skills on to a herbalist called Leung Jan Kwai who in turn taught Wong Wah Bo who worked with an opera troupe called the Red Junk. Legends abound about the Red Junk and it was there that Leung Yee Tye was introduced to the art, he was the pole man for the junk and had been shown how to use the boat's pole for fighting by one of the temple elders.

So the pole form was introduced to the system. The butterfly knives were, possibly, also introduced around the time of the Red junk.

End of 1800s

Start of more reliable documentation.

Around 100 years ago Leung Jan, a skilled physician in Fatshan, was one of the chosen few to receive training in Wing Chun. He was greatly respected by his community as a gentleman who never boasted about his kung fu. Next door to Leung lived a moneychanger by the name of Chan Wah Soon, he was a well-built martial artist who also respected his neighbour for his skills. Chan Wah Soon asked Leung Jan to teach him. Initially, Leung Jan chose to keep the art within the family.

Eventually Leung decided to teach Chan, but being a large and strong man he did not teach him in exactly the same way that he taught his sons Leung Bic and Leung Tsun, who were of smaller build and therefore needed different skills to overcome stronger opponents. Later, Leung Bic travelled to Hong Kong and Chan Wah Soon remained in Fatshan where he built up a following.

1899-1905

Amongst his students was a young boy named Yip Man. Yip Man offered Chan 300 silver pieces in return for tuition. At first Chan refused thinking the money stolen, but after a visit to the boys' parents he discovered that he had worked hard to earn the money and, being suitably impressed he took him on as a student.

Yip Man studied for four years under the instruction of Chan and after his death, following his master's wishes he continued to train under Ng Chung Sao in order to complete the system.

Why Wing Chun Works

1908

Yip Man travelled to Hong Kong to study at college. By now the young Yip Man had quite a reputation as a martial artist. Through some friends he was introduced to an eccentric old scholar renowned for his skills. The old man was no other than Leung Bic, the surviving son of Leung Jan whose father had taught him slightly different skills. Leung Bic accepted Yip Man as a student and taught him many new and different methods. In time Yip Man returned to Fatshan with his new knowledge. For the next 20 years he worked for the army and the police, he also married and had four children. The Japanese invasion of Southern China came in 1937. During these hard times he continued his training and in 1941 started to teach the first generation of students.

1948

After the war, in 1948, the communist government took over. Yip Man had to leave everything behind and go to Macao.

Eventually he returned to Hong Kong with Leung Shung, who was to become his first Hong Kong student, and set up a

Wing Chun school at the Restaurant Workers Union building, where his reputation, as both a skilful teacher of Wing Chun, and as a gentleman grew.

Yip Man's moves to Macao and then Hong Kong were very significant for the development of Wing Chun; had he remained in China, the art as it was traditionally taught may have been changed. According to contemporary research, the communists regarded martial arts as useless and outdated. They altered the content of many, adding new theatrical and acrobatic moves to enhance their appeal renaming them "Modern Wushu". The communist government infused these new arts with western competitive sporting ideals, and promoted modern Wushu, both as a means of strengthening the spirit of the socialist state, and also as a method of bringing to an end the secretive, rebellious aura that had surrounded martial arts in the past.

Over the next 22 years Yip Man taught many students, several of whom have gone on to become masters in their own right and spread the skills of Wing Chun throughout the entire world.

Why Wing Chun Works

1970s

The most famous of Yip Man's students was, of course, Bruce Lee. Lee was already well known in the East as an actor in the Hong Kong film industry. With the Hollywood blockbuster Enter The Dragon he shot to fame across the world. With the success of this film in the seventies there was an explosion of interest in kung fu and oriental culture in the West.

Yip Man passed away at his home in Hong Kong on the 1st December 1972 at the age of 79. Many of his students, and his sons, Ip Chun and Yip Ching continue to teach Wing Chun all over the world. Wing Chun still enjoys its rich heritage and history, and thanks to the endeavours and curiosity of the great number of practitioners today, it is still living, expanding and moving forward as an art, a sport, and as a way of life.

Pic 1. Grand Master Ip Chun, relaxing in his Hong Kong home.

Wing Chun Fundamental Principles

Triangulation

Wing Chun's structural strength comes from the theory of triangulation. Triangles or pyramid shapes are both strong, and easy to understand.

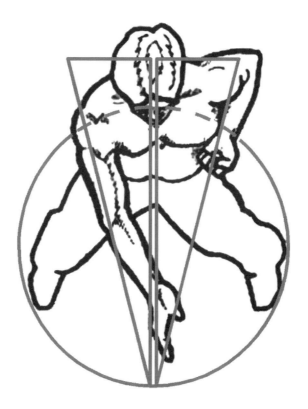

Pic 2. Looking at the body in terms of shape will make the Wing Chun principles more easy to understand and enhance learning.

Triangulation theory is easy to understand and apply because of the way our bodies are jointed. The stance is strong and stable because of its triangulation [see section on stance]; this in turn supports the upper body, which gives a firm board for the triangulated hand and arm shapes to work off.

We need to make our hand/arm shapes act like a wedge. This will cause attacks to be deflected to one side (Pic 2).

We can then think about driving this wedge into the centre [see section on centreline] or down our opponent's guard. When employed correctly, triangulation will enable our shapes to contain the strength of angles, as opposed to the over-use of muscular strength. This method is superior because it allows the limbs to remain relaxed; letting them move quickly and freely from one position to another, unhindered by muscular tension [see correct use of force].

Pivoting to return force

Physically it is necessary for the body to act like a rotating cylinder. If a force is applied to any point on its circumference it will spin in the same direction as the force. Remember though, that if one side of the cylinder rotates back, the other side is driven forward.

When a force is applied to a Wing Chun practitioner's body or arms, they should rotate, or pivot, in a similar way. As the body rotates, one side moves away from the attacker and the other moves closer (Pic 3). The counter-attack is launched from the side that moves in, utilising the movement of the bodyweight to add power to the attack. The arm that moves back is used to control the incoming attack, often a short sharp tug is used (also aided by the pivot) to unbalance the attacker and pull their arm out of the way of the counter [see Lap sau]. The pivoting action also moves the centre of gravity out of the path of the force. In this way it is possible to dispel and return a force.

When pivoting, the spine should be kept straight and upright to allow the turn to be made quickly and with precision. Short fast footwork steps can be used in the same way as the pivot, this is especially useful if the opponent is very mobile.

• The body must pivot cleanly and in a controlled way around the point of contact.

• Allow the attack to continue down its original line, only apply force to control the limb or to deflect it.

• Pivot out of the way, (choose the path of least resistance) and counter - attack down the new centre.

• Ensure that the weight is on the heels during the turn, not on the toes (this stops the body swaying about) and that the hips are kept rotated forward throughout.

Pic 3. Pivoting, and striking down a new centre. The stance turn must be fast, stable and confident. You will need to apply it under pressure.

Why Wing Chun Works

- This action is aided by keeping the head straight, hips level and rotated forward [see stance].
- If an attack is made off-centre, the direction of the pivot is obvious (move the attacked side away from the attack).
- If the attack is on centre, we can choose to pivot either way.

The final direction chosen may be influenced by other variables such as the position of the hands or feet.

Centre line theory

The pivot is made easier to understand by application of centre-line theory. This concept is (on its simplest level) an imaginary line, or plane, that extends outward from your centre in the direction that you are facing (normally towards your opponent/partner). It could also be described as the direction of your attention or intent.

When out of contact, the lead guard hand and the rear, emergency hand (Wu sau) will both lie on the centre line (Pic. 4.). This line is used to help detect, or interpret the direction of incoming forces in order to decide (feel) in which direction the pivot must occur and hence, which hand shapes are appropriate. When the centre line is defended correctly, the opponent is forced to attack along the wrong angle, in other words to the right or to the left of your centre line. This will then determine the correct defensive position or manoeuvre with which to respond. In this situation the only other alternative for an opponent is to attempt to force the centre line open using leverage or strength, however, it is possible to make use of this strength, by pivoting. Occupying the centre line also ensures that any attack you launch, will reach your opponent via the shortest possible route.

So, we must remain relaxed and fluid whilst obeying the fundamental rules, even in the face of an aggressive adversary. If we follow the rules and defend the centre successfully, opponents will become frustrated and over-commit their attacks. This in turn feeds us with the information we require to defeat them. In this way the system will still work under pressure.

Why Wing Chun Works

Pic 4 (a&b).
The centre line is an imaginary plane that moves with us.
It helps to simplify, or aim our triangulation.

When two people of similar skill levels compete, victory will rely on causing the opponent to make a mistake, either by over-committing an attack or defence, or simply by being faster or more subtle so that movement to a superior position is not detected until it is too late.

From a strong position, an attack can be launched which cannot be stopped without the use of force. If force is used to counter an attack it can quickly be capitalised upon.

Clearly it can be seen from the above that it is desirable not only to defend the centre line effectively, but also to attack on centre (not always the same as, down the centre line). This is not simply because all of the vulnerable points lie down the centre of the body.

When we strike our opponent we want the blow to have maximum effect upon them. We want all the force generated in our attack to go into them. If we want the opponent to absorb all the weight of the strike, they must not be allowed to pivot to return or dissipate its energy. This is the reason for attacking the centre.

Why Wing Chun Works

If the blow lands centrally the body soaks up all the energy and is propelled backwards, it is not able to lose any force in pivoting. It is important to notice at this point that, for an attack, the centre is a line drawn from the direction of the incoming force to the core (or spine) of the body. This is not the same as a line drawn along the front of a body unless the attack is coming straight in, square to the body (Pic 5).

The Wing Chun straight-line punch will normally land square if it comes from the inside line. However, if it comes in from outside the arm of the opponent it must hit the centre at a slight angle, allowing for the width of the attacker's shoulders, and the direction of the line into the centre of gravity. We must make sure that our energy acts through our opponent's centre of gravity. To land a glancing blow would be considered inefficient. An example of this is when a snooker or pool player wishes the cue ball to stop dead, after striking a coloured ball. The shot would have to be played square (ignoring back spin), if the coloured ball was struck at an angle the cue ball would continue to move after impact, so it has not imparted all its energy to the other ball.

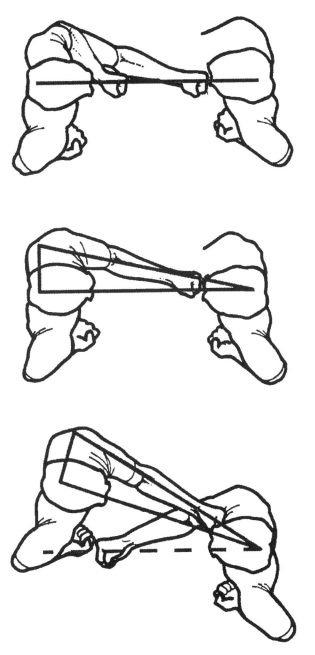

Pic 5. Strikes should be aimed at the centre of the body making it more difficult for the opponent to pivot. This allows the strike to have maximum effect.

Pic 6 (a&b). Combining the three last principles we can see that: as you pivot (or step) out of the path of an incoming attack, the counter is made on centre, and down a new line. Triangulation helps to deflect the attack whilst maintaining a strong position.

More power to your elbow

Wing Chun teachers often refer to "elbow energy" and concentrating energy at the elbow. This is a method of helping people to understand how to use the correct muscles (for maximum power) and avoid tension in the arm.

Elbow positioning is used extensively in Wing Chun to defend by deflection [see Bong sau, Fook sau and Tan sau], and to pin, trap or control an opponents limbs [see simultaneous attack and defence]. When attacking, the palm or fist is normally kept upright if it is on the inside of a limb. This has the effect of maintaining the elbow's outward leverage. If your limb is on the outside of the opponent's limb, the elbow needs to be kept in to jam the centre, this has the effect of angling the fist or palm slightly off vertical. Note the difference between the palm strikes at the end of the first, and the beginning of the third section of Siu Lim Tao.

Efficient use of energy or force

Wing Chun is well known for its speed, and ability to generate explosive power from very close (touching) range. This skill is largely down to using muscles and joints efficiently, using no more strength than is necessary to accomplish an objective.

If you ask someone to make their arm strong they will normally tense up all the muscles, both biceps and triceps, to make all the muscles bulge out. It looks and feels strong. However, because the two muscle sets actually work antagonistically, there is no useful strength there at all! We should really ask the question: Strong in which direction?

When a weight lifter performs a bench press his biceps will be totally relaxed allowing the triceps and pectorals to have maximum effect. It follows that the Wing Chun punch does not use the biceps, except to stop the arm extending too far and to make minute adjustments. Any opposing tension in the upper arm would slow down the dynamic action of the punch.

The position of the elbow, which drives the punch forward, (in alignment with the shoulder, wrist and knuckles) and the application of energy, or tension, at the moment of impact, also helps to achieve a clean transfer of energy into the opponent. Immediately afterwards the arm must return to its relaxed state. This correct and efficient use of muscles and joint angles should be studied in the forms [see Siu Lim Tao] and used in every technique and position.

Short Force and the Inch Punch

Wing Chun is legendary for its Inch Force. As mentioned previously, the arms need to be relaxed in order to be able to change shape or direction quickly. So the ability to switch on instant power from any position, and from touching range is vital.

With correct training, it is not difficult to master inch force in a fairly short time. However, it is important to understand where the power for the strike is coming from in order to be able to improve [see also chapter on stance]. A simple and systematic approach to practice will help to train the correct body habits.

Why Wing Chun Works

If you achieve correct muscle tension, joint alignment and stance movement, you will hit with the weight of your moving body, as opposed to just the weight and speed of your limb.

Using the stance to help you hit will ensure maximum power with minimum commitment. Your legs are strong enough to carry and move your body weight forward, thus adding impetus to your strike. Understanding the connection between the ground and your strike is very important [see stance].

Learning to punch

1. Start by training the ability to accelerate the hand from a relaxed, bent arm position. The hand should be open; the elbow should be kept low (in line with the arm). Do not pull back before punching, and do not move the body (maintain a fixed stance). The movement should end relaxed, and in the finished punch position (Pic 7).

2. Next learn to tense the fist at the end of the movement, ensuring that the bottom two knuckles finish pronounced,

and driven from the elbow. The fingers should 'roll up' as the hand travels forward.

3. Train the body to move behind the punch. This can be done by pivoting from a square stance or by stepping from a forward stance. A wall bag is a very useful tool here, to make sure that you are not losing any power at the joints (wrist, elbow or shoulder), or bouncing back off the target.

4. Practice on a consenting partner, or again on the wall bag. If you use a partner, be sure to use a suitable protector (improvisation is possible with a telephone directory or thick book placed on the chest) to spread the impact out and prevent bruising. Starting with your fingers touching the pad, and not pulling back first, practise your punch. Imagine that the target is simply not there at all, and carry out a fast relaxed punch, exactly as you would in the air. Visualise your punch carrying through to completion and the final position with the fist tensed.

Pic. 7 (a&b). Learn to accelerate the punch rapidly from the elbow. Keep the limb totally relaxed at first, then begin to tense the fist at the very end of the movement. The arm should bounce back in a natural way.

Helpful Hints

• Do not push your partner, although this may help to get the idea in the early stages.

• Do not aim to hit at the surface of the padding.

• Your punch should go through all the stages it would in the air, it will help if you can gain feedback from an experienced practitioner.

• When you start to get it right, make sure any demonstration is practised safely, i.e. consenting adults and not in front of glass doors or other dangerous objects (it is entirely possible to send the person back several metres, or for them to be knocked down).

• Immediately after punching your arm and fist should be relaxed again, enabling it to hit again, or perform another operation [see use of force].

The inch palm is similar in its application, but you must aim to drive the heel of the palm from the elbow.

This can also be practised on a wall bag. Drop your weight into the target with a slight pivot. Alternatively, use a short, sharp push from your stance, striking slightly upwards at the same time. Do not bounce back, or lose energy in the joints. If you do not have a wall bag you can practise (carefully) on sturdy walls or swing doors. You will be able to feel your body weight jolting when the technique is correct.

It is possible to deliver inch force from most major joints including; the elbows, shoulders, feet, knees and even the hips.

Simplicity

Another aspect that contributes to the success of Wing Chun is its simplicity: rather than employ a large amount of different techniques, Wing Chun practitioners strive to understand thoroughly, the variety of ways in which a few, simple techniques can be adapted to deal with many different situations.

The fundamental positions are given in the third section of the first form Siu Lim Tao (the little idea) which relates to the single sticking hands exercise. These ideas are then expanded upon in the second form Chum Kiu (searching for the bridge) where pivoting, stepping and kicking are introduced, along with the simultaneous use of both hands, leading to the lap sau exercise.

Chi sau then allows us to fully explore all the possible combinations and varieties of technique, whilst in motion. This systematic (modular) learning process gives students easily understandable targets to aim at. As one level is absorbed it is then integrated and expanded upon.

The most frequently occurring shapes are: Bong sau, Tan sau, and Fook sau (Pic 8).

Basic Shapes

Bong sau (wing arm)

Bong sau is a soft shape, and the forearm must contain no strength (keep the fingers relaxed). The muscles of the shoulder are required to hold the elbow in position, the upper arm should be parallel to the centre line, and the defending elbow must be higher than the attacking elbow.

Why Wing Chun Works

Bong sau works by collapsing inward from the upturned elbow, or by wedging in to jam the centre. As the practitioner pivots into the incoming force, the aggressor is deflected, or allowed to over commit. The final position of this Bong sau leaves us in a prime position for performing a Lap sau, or punching from the Wu sau (Pic 9)

Pic. 8. Basic Wing Chun Shapes; Bong sau, Tan sau, and Fook sau. Pivot to deflect the attack, whilst maintaining centre.

Bong sau will work from the outside line (right Bong left arm), or from the inside line (right Bong right arm). On the inside line, care must be taken to prevent the elbow from being pinned.

Bong sau can also be used as a bridge to obtain contact. Application would be the same as in the second section of the second form (Chum kiu). Here the Bong sau can be sent forward to seek the arm of an attacker as the defender steps out of the line of attack. A sideways step should be used as the Bong sau is sent forward to meet the arm. As contact is made the Bong sau arm can be used to perform Lap sau, or to control the limb.

These Bong sau applications use different positioning and energies, giving different perspectives on the centre line, it is useful to experiment and become familiar with both of them.

Pic. 9. Bong sau defends by elbow positioning. Here, Wu sau is available to perform Lap sau, or to punch.

Tan sau (palm up block)

Tan sau is a very strong shape, and can be considered as the opposite of Bong sau. (Pic. 10.) It is driven forward from the elbow, with energy supplied by the triceps and inner deltoid muscle, making it very strong down its length. The biceps muscle is used to turn the palm upwards and outwards. Tan sau also, is often in a good position to lead into a Lap sau, or Pak sau technique.

Pic. 10. Tan sau defending on the inside or outside line, as the free hand punches the centre.

Tan sau will work on the inside line (right Tan left arm), or on the outside (right Tan right arm).

Any excessive force across Tan sau (or across the centre line), should still cause it to collapse, or roll over into another shape, like Bong sau.

Note in this case, that the practitioner's arm is on the inside at first, and finishes on the outside; contact and control has not been lost at any point during this change. This combination of movements could also be considered in reverse, with the Bong sau corkscrewing forward into Tan sau.

Fook sau (bridge on arm)

Fook sau is used to control the position of an opponent's arm from the outside gate. The energy should again be concentrated in the elbow and upper forearm. The hand should not push down or across. Once again elbow position is used to control the centre line. As an incoming force is detected, the practitioner pivots to a position of safety, behind the elbow. (Pic. 11.) If a free hand is available this move facilitates Lap sau, Jut sau or Pak sau.

Pic. 11. Fook sau, used for controlling an opponent's limb from the outside line.

Why Wing Chun Works

Fook sau can also 'evolve', or roll into other hand shapes, such as Jum sau [see single sticking hands], or Huen sau (circling hand). Once again, control and contact must be maintained throughout these transitions. Other shapes, such as Gong sau (Pic. 12), can also be used from the outside line.

(Pic. 12.) Gong sau can also be used to subdue an attack from the outside line.

Wing Chun defence revolves around these shapes, and it is essential to gain an in-depth understanding of them; this means not only how and when to apply them but also how they can evolve from one to another, how and when tension is used during these changes and how stepping or turning can alter the effect they have.

A clear understanding of the many different ways in which these shapes can be used will result in proficient and effective Wing Chun. This may seem to be an over simplification, but to fully understand and master the many subtle aspects of these three shapes can take a lifetime.

Note also that any time a hand is not performing a task it is normally held in the Wu sau (guard hand) position. Wu sau lies on the centre line, covering the chin throat or nose in case any attacks penetrate the defence. Wu sau is also a position of readiness, the hand can spring out from the centre to attack, or take on any other shape.

The Wing Chun practitioner aims to achieve a position of superior strength and angle with every single move. During any defence, attack, footwork-step or posture shift, the centre line must be tightly controlled, thus maintaining the opponent's disadvantage and forcing them to attack/defend from a poor angle.

In training each move can be treated as an individual step and potential choices can be analysed in simple stages. Once the best option is selected, the appropriate responses can then be drilled in and finally joined up into a string of individual techniques that flow from one into another. The teaching of correct positioning and range can be difficult; a clear understanding of posture, hand shapes and the centre line needs to be gained first, then through gradual experimentation in Chi sau, positioning can be properly understood.

Another aspect of simplicity in the system is that in Wing Chun the aim is to find and occupy the centre. One goal is to be achieved and the global idea is simple.

Contact Reflexes

Due to the in-contact, reactionary nature of Wing Chun, [see also drills] techniques are quickly programmed into the subconscious mind of the practitioner, and become reflexive (bypassing the conscious thought process). This enables the practitioner to react far faster than would be possible with a visual reflex. The correct reflex is instantaneous.

Contact reflexes also give the mind more time to concentrate on other aspects, like strategy, and the attainment of higher levels of skill. Without the use of this method, the practitioner would have to retain and choose from a vast store of information about all the possible variations of attack. It would be necessary to see and understand the nature of each attack, choose an appropriate defence and then act accordingly. This is not necessary with a contact reflex so the selection process is far faster.

The theory and process of autonomous reflex actions are not yet completely understood. It is believed that learned subconscious reflexes (including every day movements like walking, driving a car, or riding a bicycle) are programmed into either the brain or the spinal cord.

Research has shown that there are two levels of movement programming in the body: one level for choosing the correct pattern of activities, and another level for actually controlling and producing the patterns as they unfold. The practitioner can pre-program the details of the movement in advance [see drills] and simply wait for the reaction signal to trigger the action.

The exercises and drills of Wing Chun train the arms and hands to act as sensors to enable us to feel the direction, strength and speed of forces. The movements and hand shapes that we use are a direct result of our opponent's actions; so it is necessary for our shapes to fit around them as they move. And remember, the movement involved in making the change from one position to the next is just as important as the final position.

Our arms and body must also act as shock absorbers. It is possible that a movement may be too fast for us to react to, or so insignificant, that reaction is not merited. In these cases we need to buffer ourselves, until such a time, as we can be clear about what is happening, and react appropriately.

It is also possible, momentarily, to hold onto a force or store it up before unleashing it back down a different line. This could be likened to a bowstring or catapult being drawn before the projectile is released toward the target. It is, however, worth noting that it is considered more efficient and skilful to react immediately and cleanly.

The ability to achieve these levels of subtlety and skill is attained by training in the Wing Chun drills, and through the practice of sticking hands or Chi sau.

Simultaneous attack and defence

Simultaneous attack and defence does not only mean doing one thing with one hand (defending), and something different with the other (attacking). In Wing Chun this happens most of the time. Simultaneous attack and defence also refers to one hand serving two purposes at once.

Why Wing Chun Works

By defending the centre line, rather than chasing the hands of an opponent, it is possible to deflect an attack and launch an assault on the opponent's centre at the same time, with only one arm. Frequently the situation arises where the elbow is pinning an arm down whilst the hand and wrist are still free to attack the centre. Tan-Biu sau in Chum Kiu form is a good example of this. Bong sau can also be turned into a short elbow strike, simply by closing down the range, and applying the correct energy.

Importance of stance and posture

The Wing Chun stance is frequently misunderstood because, at first glance and when first practised, it seems to be extraordinarily awkward and immobile. However, as with many other aspects of the art, once the mechanics and theory have been understood, it starts to make a lot more sense.

Understanding the relationship between the ground (or our feet), and our hands, is of vital importance to freedom of movement, and also, our ability to attack strongly and defend effectively. Clearly the two are connected but we need to establish exactly what happens when we arrive in a position, how different stances benefit certain situations and how we can move fluidly from one position to another without getting trapped in a particular stance.

Boxers understand the mechanics involved in hitting off the floor, gaining power by rotating the trunk and developing speed by accelerating the shoulder joint forward. Karate practitioners use a twist of the hips to generate power. Wing Chun uses the stance and footwork to develop tremendous speed, accuracy and power without over-committing the body weight (compromising balance).

We have already discussed pivoting to return a force, and the correct use of energy and elbow leverage, but these points are useless without a stable and mobile base for them to work off.

Any fixed stance is only strong in two directions, so it is important to understand how to aim it correctly, and to be able to move quickly and naturally from one position to another. We need a leg behind in order to push forward, and also to be able to withstand incoming force, without pivoting or leaning. We also need a leg in front to prevent our being pulled or over-committing with our weight.

The normal, Wing Chun square stance is strong for receiving sideways stress. This is why the early stages of Wing Chun training emphasise triangulation, using shapes that are able to collapse inward, or across the body with the aid of a pivot. As an attack comes in, we must turn to face the direction from which it is coming. It is vital to maintain optimum strength of posture at all times. Our stance needs to be strong in the right direction.

Stepping and turning should be as natural as walking to the Wing Chun practitioner. You must be able to move through stances, steps and kicks whilst maintaining perfect distance (Bruce Lee was the Cha Cha dance champion of Hong Kong), no matter what the opponent does. Remember that your range and positioning will change according to your stance and arm shapes. Practising Chum kiu, the wooden dummy form and Chi sau, will help train an understanding of footwork.

Another point to address is the position of the feet; some people advocate the knees and toes turned in, whilst others say they should be parallel. The difference is that if the toes are turned in you can pivot by only moving one foot. Leaving the back foot stationary whilst pivoting, could arguably give a more solid base.

If the feet are kept parallel it is necessary to turn both feet simultaneously in order to pivot. This gives a slightly different feel to the turn. Experimentation in the drills, and in Chum Kiu form will determine which is preferable, and under what conditions each is appropriate.

During any pivoting action it is important to keep the weight on the heels (Pic.13.), this is aided by keeping the head back and the spine straight (look down your nose at your opponent!). The knees must be kept in alignment with the feet. This will avoid any sideways stress on the knee joint, and prevent locking out. This action also helps to cover the groin.

The pelvis must be rotated forwards, and kept level during the turn (allowing you to push without committing your weight). The point of balance should be mid way between the feet in a normal stance. The stance should feel springy and mobile, not stiff and restrictive.

Notice that after turning we are, effectively, in a forward stance, facing sideways (depending on where the centre line is). The turn, like every other aspect of the art needs to be sensitive to force. Any intended pivot can, and must be, changed or abandoned as circumstances dictate.

As far as possible, initial movement in the upper body must be created from the feet, knees and hips (and the waist beyond 45 degrees) not at the back or shoulders, which may cause us to lose our triangulation.

When closing down to attack, the weight should be kept between the legs, allowing for strong easy movement.

The rear leg is our connection with the ground allowing us to press forwards or upwards, to accelerate and to absorb incoming forces or pressure. The front leg prevents us from being pulled forward, or our arms from being pulled down.

Why Wing Chun Works

Pic. 13 (a&b).Keep your weight central and over the heels, do not lean back. If you turn on the toes your body will swing about, making precision movement impossible. Also you will not be able to press the centre without commitment.

The lead leg also acts as brake when we go forward, stopping over-committing during an advance, and can be used to push off if we need to move backwards or change direction. The strength of any strike, or defence depends to a large extent on the stability of the stance. Without a strong stance we do not have a solid base to hit from.

The power of a strike relies on speed, movement of bodyweight and technique. Weight cannot be changed. Speed can be developed, with the correct use and training of the muscles. But technique can be improved dramatically by a thorough understanding of where power comes from in the stance. The ability to utilise our body weight comes from the ground because we push against it with our feet and legs. To understand this more clearly try this simple exercise:

Stance testing

In a basic stance get a partner to push against your Tan sau and feel the force being absorbed in your stance (Pic. 14).

Pic. 14. Stance dynamics. Pushes and pulls can be resisted if the stance is strong in the right direction.

Similarly, you can try pushing a punch up and out against pressure from a partner (Pic. 15.). This will test the stability and effectiveness of your structure. If the arm is suddenly released, it can spring forward into a punch. The left foot acts as a stop to prevent committed forward motion of the body. The spring in the rear leg is rocked into the front leg and bounced up through the arm.

Pic. 15. Push against a punch to test structure.

Why Wing Chun Works

Then get your partner to pull forward on your Tan sau or on the back of your neck. Do not allow your body to tip forward, or turn. Feel the pressure going into your front leg. Pull back, wedging your feet against the ground as in a tug of war. If the stance starts to tip over, take a small step forward and reassert your front leg, shuffling the rear leg up to adjust the posture.

Pic. 16a 16b 16c. Do not allow the stance to be compromised by bending at the waist.

When moving, the legs should remain springy and act like shock absorbers, but you should attempt to remain at a constant height neither bobbing up and down, nor attempting to reach over an opponent's guard to hit them. Try instead to act (using triangulation) like a wedge that is slotted in towards the opponent's centre causing them to use force to prevent the attack.

Footwork

When changing from a square stance to a forward stance (Pic. 17.), it is important to remember that by pushing from the stationary leg, it is possible to step into an opponent or alter your position, without an initial step, or shift of the weight. This enables you to make a significant shift of position without telegraphing intentions to your opponent. Pushing from the front leg will also strengthen your technique as you retreat under pressure.

The circle step found in Biu Tze also enables you to move in and trip or trap an opponent's stance. This manoeuvre is also

Why Wing Chun Works

useful if you wish to strike (using, for instance, Pak sau) but the angle, or range is not right to launch an attack.

Pic. 17 (a&b). Pushing off the rear leg enables us to step directly, with no preparatory movement.

Why Wing Chun Works

Some practitioners have abandoned the traditional leg forward footwork and chosen to step in a lateral or circular pattern, not unlike the foot work of the Pa Kua styles. As an opponent moves in to attack, instead of pivoting the defender steps forward at an angle of 45 degrees, rather like a tennis player receiving a serve. Moving around the attack has a dissipating effect, not unlike that experienced by pivoting, it is possible to move larger distances and, perhaps, be a little more mobile from the initial start position [see bridging].

This lateral footwork is also particularly useful when you are under pressure from a forward pressing attack, allowing the defender to slip to the side, dropping a strike in as they move. It must be remembered though, that whilst lateral footwork is very mobile side to side, it is not so practical if you wish to pursue a retreating person, or pressure an opponent. This is because it is not possible to apply any forward pressure without leaning in, causing over-commitment (step in, to change to a forward stance).

Kicking and sweeping

Whilst spending much of the time with two feet firmly on, or close to the ground, the Wing Chun practitioner must also understand how and when to kick effectively. Before learning how to kick, the basic stances, steps, and turns, must be learned in order to achieve a proper understanding of balance, and the dynamics of the legs and hips.

All the Wing Chun kicks are found in Chum Kiu and the wooden dummy form. They are sometimes known as shadowless kicks. They are swift direct and low, targets include the feet, shins, knees (front, back and side), thighs, groin and hips.

Wing Chun kicks rarely land higher than the waist. The reason for their speed and subtlety is that they work on the same principle as the hands, i.e. they usually travel straight to the target without needing to be chambered or drawn back first. Whilst performing a front kick, the hips remain rotated forward and at more or less the same angle.

Pic. 18. Kicking from a pivot or Lap sau.

The percussive force of the kick comes from acceleration of the leg and from pushing up from the ground, in this way, any recoil is sent back into the stance. If you kick downwards, any forceful collision can disrupt your posture and cause imbalance.

The force with which the Wing Chun kicks strike the target is similar to that of the inch punch, only heavier; likewise there should be no over commitment. Often the front kick will be performed from a pivot, either stamping or hacking.

Pic. 19. Using a side kick to prevent an arm lock.

Why Wing Chun Works

The foot can follow the same route as it would in a circle step, only with the foot turned out and tensioned back. The kick gains dynamic torque from the circle, whilst not telegraphing the movement through the hands due to its path through the centre of gravity.

Sometimes kicks will be the result of exaggerated footwork manoeuvres or hand techniques such as Lap sau; again this makes them difficult to detect (Pic. 18).

If the posture is disrupted a kick can be used to right the situation. If the posture is broken backwards a lifting front kick can be employed, if you are attacked from, or out flanked a side kick will be appropriate. A side kick is also a useful way to free off some arm locks. (Pic. 19.)

The most important things to remember about kicking are to remain stable, balanced and above all, be in control of the opponent before unleashing the attack. Hence the saying, If you want to kick like a mule keep three legs on the ground! (Two of theirs and one of yours). Also when kicking we need to know what to kick at: the simple answer is to kick at the target that is nearest, or most appropriate at the given time, and as with the hands, be prepared to change with the circumstances.

Often a sharp tug forwards and downwards will bring a limb into range for kicking, it will also put the opponent's weight onto the limb, this will make it a better target due to its load bearing nature. If there is any doubt or instability in the situation, keep your feet firmly on the ground and continue to control with the hands.

Defending against kicks

Prevention of, and defence against, kicks, can be achieved in several different ways; first comes proximity and pressure. Many martial artists and for that matter other fighters, do not feel comfortable with the range that Wing Chun employs and certainly cannot kick effectively from it. If the opponent attempts to gain distance, simply follow them back applying pressure all the while.

Pic. 20. Kicking into a round-kick.

"Kick a kicker" is another phrase that springs to mind here. In other words if an opponent attempts to kick you from close range, as soon as his leg leaves the ground (this can be felt and trained for in Chi sau or Chi gerk), pick your own lead leg up, preventing it being trapped against the ground and kick the supporting leg (or the kicking leg) of your opponent away. (Pics. 20 & 21.)

Pic. 21. Kicking a kicker as the foot leaves the ground.

Other equally effective defences are the use of Gum sau or Gaun sau to cover the lower areas. Or just a simple tug on the arm in the appropriate direction (often downwards) as the foot leaves the ground. This has an unbalancing effect causing the body's natural defence mechanisms to put the foot quickly back onto the ground in order to prevent the person falling over.

Why Wing Chun Works

If an opponent attempts to perform a foot sweep on your lead leg it needs to be able to return to centre, in the same way that a hand would, and immediately attack their load bearing leg. Often a kick can be used in conjunction with the hands either as a trip, a distraction technique or (very usefully) as a method of creating an off-centre force in the hands, which can then be capitalised upon in the usual way.

Most of these skills can be practised in Chi gerk or sticky legs or even in combination with Chi sau but care must be taken to ensure that these skills are practised under controlled conditions, heavy kicks to vulnerable parts such as the knees are dangerous. Also if you always kick in Chi sau there will be a tendency to neglect training the hands.

Bridging the gap

As mentioned previously the advantage that a Wing Chun practitioner gains over others is the ability to deal with situations from a position of contact. Once this is gained it must not be lost. Another advantage is that the range that Wing Chun employs tends to be too close for most others;

causing them to retreat, and us to follow, applying pressure all the time. However, not all situations will occur from a convenient initial position of close contact.

In these instances we need to employ a method of obtaining contact, preferably without getting hit! It is important to remember at this point, that the primary aim is to gain contact and find the centre, from thereon in our contact reflexes and sticking hands skills will take over.

We need to move (pivot or step depending on the attack) out of the way of the attack but at the same time gently gain contact in order to understand how to deal with it. Mun sau (asking hand) is often considered a suitable method of gaining contact (If you don't ask you don't get!). Treat every attack with a healthy respect, aim to intercept it smoothly, as you would if you were attempting to catch a hard object such as a cricket ball or a fragile one like an egg.

Once contact has been obtained we can tell how sticky, fast, strong or tense our opponent is and so determine how best to deal with them. The simplest way of achieving this is to set the guard angled slightly off centre; this will encourage an attack down a predicted line. As the attack comes in, move to the chosen side by use of a lateral step.

The bridging hand is fired into the centre, or sometimes toward the opposite shoulder. On the inside line, you will need to stop the upper-arm moving, or stop the body rotating (Pic. 22.). It will help to watch the movement of the elbow, as this travels more slowly than the hand, and is a better position for controlling the body's movement from. Once contact has been gained reflexes should be the same as would be achieved through Chi sau practice.

It is possible to bridge using any appropriate hand shapes e.g. Bong sau, Tan sau, Gaun sau, Gum sau etc. With practice against a variety of different attacks, you will soon discover which method suits each situation, but you must be prepared to ad lib to some extent in order to find a smooth and safe way of gaining contact before moving into hand techniques.

Do not forget, the aim is to gain contact and control, in order to find centre. To achieve this safely your footwork will need to be very mobile and able to change direction quickly (well balanced). Think about a tennis player waiting to receive a service, or remember playing tag at school, it really is not that different.

Pic. 22. Bridging. Close down the attack, gain contact and hit the centre.

The Wing Chun Drills

The Wing Chun system has several unique drills. They are performed in contact, and are cyclic, to allow simple repetitions and variations. The purpose of these drills is to program an appropriate response into the body's reflex system [see contact reflexes].

Some of the drills have a set pattern of movements but the techniques need to be responsive and not a premeditated anticipation. To this end once the basic drills have been understood, they can be varied and adapted according to a specific concept. Cyclic drills are not hard to make up once the basic ideas are absorbed and they can be a very effective way of accelerating learning without fighting. Eventually the drills should blend in with and become an integral part of Chi sau practice.

Single Sticking Hands (Dan Chi Sau)

Single sticking hands provides beginners with a simple but excellent drill to practice, and leads to an understanding of the basic principles. In the first instance it is necessary to have a good stance and posture, leading to an understanding of how to apply good technique from a stable base. Students learn to stick to a partner's arm in order to feel their intention. One person will attack, in a given pattern (Tan sau into straight palm), and the partner learns the skill of dissolving (Fook sau into Jum sau) and returning the attack (centre punch). As the attack is returned the original attacker will feel the movement and defend (Bong sau). The cycle of movements is then repeated (Pic. 23).

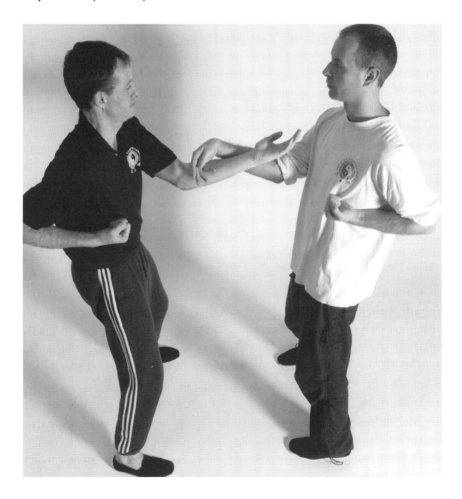

It is vital that the sequence does not become too predictable, so it is useful to try to catch your partner out by getting into a rhythm, then breaking it and seeing if they are really responding to your attacks. If their defensive movements are

Pic. 23 (a,b&c). Single Sticking Hands.

the result of pre-meditation you should be able to feel them start to defend fractionally before your attack and by suddenly not attacking they will be left in a useless position.

Why Wing Chun Works

It is important to let the limbs operate independently and the techniques should not cause the body to wobble about. Learn how to drive each strike from the elbow, not the fist or palm. The stance is also trained here, using the legs to generate strength by pushing up off the floor rather than leaning in. Other skills that are learned in single sticking hands include: centre line control, correct use of energy, and elbow leverage or triangulation (by positioning the joints at an appropriate angle and using muscles efficiently optimum strength is achieved with a minimum of effort). Simple hand changes can be introduced once the cycle has been learned (see hand changes). This will also help to build in the concept of the hand smoothly returning to centre when forced off. The idea of Lut sau (hand free hit centre) can also be introduced at this stage, if one partner suddenly removes their hand from the drill, or over-commits in defence, the other's now free hand should shoot forward instantly, to attack the centre.

Later it is possible to practise single sticking hands diagonally, or with the introduction of the pivot and footwork. All of these skills will be needed later in Chi sau (Double sticking hands), so it is highly beneficial to practise and understand the concepts at this early stage.

Lap sau and Pac sau

Lap sau and Pac sau are the fundamental Wing Chun techniques of attack; they can also be used to control and to defend. It is essential for the practitioner to spend plenty of time with these ideas and to get familiar with the variety of ways in which they can be used. Literally translated Lap sau means pulling arm, Pac sau means slap block, and on a basic level this is how these techniques are applied.

Pic. 24. Lap sau technique, with a punch.

Why Wing Chun Works

Lap sau

Lap sau is used when the lead arm is in contact with the opponent's limb, and we want to attack with the rear hand. The arm is given a short, sharp tug, normally in a downward direction. At the same time, an attack is launched from the other hand. The opponent's arm is pulled out of the way, and they are pulled onto the attack (Pic. 24). Lap sau is often performed from a pivot.

Lap sau drill

Lap sau drill is cyclic; one person performs a Lap sau technique with a punch from a square stance, the partner pivots on the centre using Bong sau (the drill can be practised square on as well). The defender then performs Lap sau and punches with their Wu sau hand, whilst returning to the original centre. The original attacker then pivots off to Bong. This process is then repeated (Pic. 25).

A change of sides can be obtained if the defender, using the hand of his Bong sau arm, grasps and pulls the arm that has just performed Lap sau on him.

It is important to remain relaxed throughout the drill. You must take care not to over commit with either Bong sau or the punch and be mindful of where the centre is at all times. When performing Lap sau, it is good to vary the speed and strength of your technique. This will test your partners Bong sau. It is easy to devise variations and interruptions to the Lap sau drill. These changes will encourage improvisation and enable the development of a more rounded skill.

Pic. 25 (a,b&c). Lap sau drill, showing a change of sides.

Pac sau

Pac sau means slap block; it is a short percussive palm strike or press toward the opposite shoulder. Pac sau can be used as a non-committal blocking move, or it can be used to move a limb to facilitate an attack from the other hand. Normally the attack would be launched from the lead hand (Pic 26).

Pic. 26. Pak sau and punch from the rear hand.

Why Wing Chun Works

As we have seen, if you apply excessive force to a skilful opponent they will interpret and recycle your energy to use against you. If you use either Lap or Pac sau techniques in a clumsy or unsuitable way they are simple to defend against. Do not think of them merely as a means of removing an obstacle from the path of your attacking hand because they can be of so much more use. If you make an attack when you are in contact with an arm or hand your opponent will be able to feel the attack and if they are skilful they will be successful in defence. Pak sau and Lap sau can both be used to unstick a potential attack from a defender's arm, changing the perspective of a situation in an instant from; Hand comes detain (for the defender), to Hand free hit centre (for the attacker).

These techniques can also be used to change an attack from one side of the body to the other, from inside to outside gate (and vice versa) and to obtain contact with the other (rear) hand. Pac sau can be quickly followed by Lap sau, and Lap sau can be changed into Pac sau half way through.

As a rule the safest and cleanest attacks will be the result of Pac sau or Lap sau. The only other legitimate times to attack are in the situation of 'hand free hit' or when an opponent's hand has left the area you need to defend and you are able to slip through an ineffective defence. Most cases of over commitment or excessive use of force will result in Lap sau or Pac sau situations.

When practising Lap sau as a cyclic drill, try not to always count the rhythm as, one - for your Bong sau defence and then, two -for your centre punch attack. Sometimes it pays to think of the Bong sau and retaliation as one whole move. In this way you will develop the good habit of tagging an attack straight on to the end of a defence, with no gap.

Chi Sau: The heart and soul of Wing Chun

Double sticking hands

Chi sau is one of the fundamental reasons why Wing Chun is so different from all other martial arts. No other martial arts have a training exercise to equal the speed at which extremely high levels of skill can be learned.

Why Wing Chun Works

Tai Chi, and some Kung fu groups, practice a pushing hands drill (akin to single sticking hands in Wing Chun). This exercise only involves the use of one hand or side at a time [see single sticking hands] and is therefore teaching a different skill. (In Chi sau both hands are working simultaneously) The unique exercise of Chi Sau teaches us to be sensitive to the smallest movements of our opponent and to react in accordance with exactly what is happening.

We are always very aware of where our hands are relative to our bodies, (we rarely hit ourselves accidentally). The hands or wrists are in contact with the opponent's; we therefore know instinctively where our opponent's hands are, so it becomes a relatively simple matter to stop them from hitting us.

The forearms hands and fingers are very sensitive to movement and can be taught control in a very subtle way. When we pick up a delicate object up we do not use the same force necessary to pick up, for instance, a sack of potatoes. We only grip as firmly as we need to, if something slips, feedback through the nervous system automatically tells us to grip more firmly or change our position. Chi sau operates largely on this subconscious level.

The purpose of Chi sau is to provide a learning link between the forms and fighting. It quickly teaches us how to apply the random techniques of free fighting in an environment of safety and learning. Risk of injury is slight as Chi sau is a learning process and not a fight.

Learning research has shown that random practice is far more effective than practising prearranged sets of movements. Drills can be learned in Chi sau but also it is used to experiment and ad lib. You never know what to expect, and must learn to feel attacks in order to defend correctly. Also, there is little evidence that the conditions under which a skill is learned need to replicate those in which they will eventually be used. This means that you don't need to fight whilst practising chi sau, in order to learn effective skill.

It is apparent that chi sau requires focused concentration, and considerable skill. At first this will be difficult because the student is trying to interpret a situation that is constantly changing and using hand shapes that they may not be totally familiar with. To enable a student to get used to the process there are several simplified exercises that can be practised [see previous chapters].

Once these skills have been mastered, students progress to Poon sau (rolling arms). This introduces the basic shapes of Chi sau; Bong, Tan, and Fook sau, without technique, from here the hand changes can be learned and the student progresses naturally onto full Chi sau. Poon sau is a part of full Chi sau training, but it is also used as a neutral gear, between techniques (Pic. 27).

Hand Changes in Chi Sau

Once a student has learned simple rolling arms (Poon sau) to develop sensitivity in the shapes, the next step towards Chi sau is to learn how to move a hand smoothly from the inside to the outside and vice versa. This skill relies heavily on timing and will also teach an awareness of this.

The movement of the hand as it changes is similar to that of Huen sau, the hand rolls around to the opposite side of the arm pivoting about the wrist. Timing is crucial as the change must begin at the top or bottom of the roll and be completed in time with it, so as not to be easily detected.

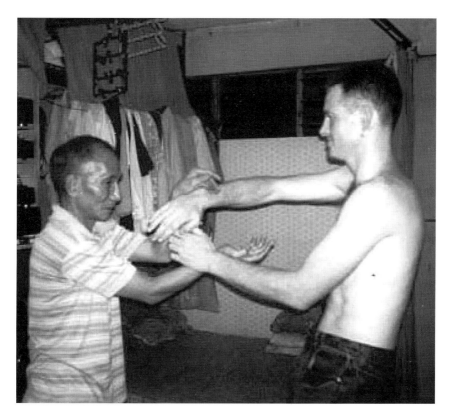

Pic. 27. The author practising Poon sau or rolling arms with Grandmaster Ip Chun 1993

Why Wing Chun Works

In a change from outside to inside, the Fook sau rolls inside, under the arm, and into Tan sau, causing the opponent to move to Fook sau to prevent being hit. In a change from inside to outside the Tan sau rolls underneath the arm, and into Fook sau or Gaun sau causing a corresponding change in the opponent. When making a change it is important to maintain contact with the wrist if possible.

Push hand changes and free hands

It is also possible to integrate a different system of force sensitive hand changes into Chi sau. Using the idea that when a hand is pushed off the centre it must return to it as smoothly and swiftly as possible, the Chi sau hand changes can be applied as the result of very slight off centre force.

These rolls back to centre can be taught out of rolling arms or Chi sau on individual hands at first but should be integrated as soon as the student is familiar with the rolling arms. The hand changes will move an arm from the inside to the outside and vice versa.

As the hands change sides and return to centre they must also be feeling gently towards the centre. In the early stages of learning the student must learn to react to any force that pushes the hand out or down from the centre causing the hand to roll back in. Once this skill has been attained they must then learn to produce changes in their partner by pushing slightly off centre, deliberately, then sticking to their partner's hand as it returns to prevent being hit themselves. After a period of co-operative practice you will soon find that it is possible to change sides in a smooth, economical and gap free manner.

At first, skill in Chi sau is more a matter of knowing how to correct errors. In the early stages this can be more realistic than expecting to get every move 100% correct all of the time, as this assumes the aggressor has no skill at all. Remember, if force is used, a skilled opponent will make use of it against you. Often an inexperienced opponent will quickly become frustrated and produce an over-committed attack, thus enabling the practitioner to redirect the force and counter from a different angle.

Why Wing Chun Works

It is also useful to introduce at this stage the idea of Hand free hit centre. The easiest way to learn this important skill is to have a Chi sau partner quickly take out one hand at random times during training. As soon as your hand is free from its sticking duties it should spring, or fall into the gap, and swiftly move to the centre, there should be no preparation or hesitation. Here, as always, it is vital that the student ensures that any forward movement of the arms is relaxed, springy and not committed. It is quite easy to ensure this by interrupting, or blocking some, but not all, of the shots that fall into the centre.

Defending in Chi sau is a matter of maintaining a superior position and controlling the centre line; it is important to redirect the opponent's attack [see pivoting] and not to use excessive force in controlling it. If force is used, a skilled opponent will feel the block as it happens, make use of the energy and return the blow from another angle.

It is a useful practise to slow Chi sau right down and view individual moves frame by frame, with one person attacking, the other defending. If an attack is successful or proves awkward to defend, you can rewind and try different methods until an appropriate move is found. Once the best option is discovered, the move can then be sped up and drilled until it becomes natural. This is an effective method of improving positioning and the understanding of how simple footwork and hand shapes can work in many different ways. If you always practise at speed you will never see all the options that are available, and will often use strength or speed to correct simple errors that should have been avoided in the first place. Your skill will be increased by patient critical analysis.

The aim in Wing Chun is to be as efficient as possible, achieving the best results, with the minimum of effort. Lao Tzu the great Taoist sage told us: "The wise man does nothing, and everything gets done". To this end it is necessary for the arms to be relaxed when they are in motion, this will enable them to change shape in a fast yet fluid way. Tension is only introduced momentarily, usually on the impact of a strike, or on arrival at a specific position. After a blow is landed the limb is returned to its relaxed state immediately, thus allowing continuing movement.

Attacking moves must be sent forward in a non-committed, relaxed way, as soon as the attack deviates from the centre, or the angle is covered, it must be abandoned or changed. Do not try to force a line, instead change angle, or change shape. The fact that an attack did not get through should indicate that a change is due (these changes of angle can and frequently will occur several times per second during sticking hands practice).

Other advantages of staying relaxed during training include being more likely to use the correct muscles [see use of energy] and less likely to suffer from fatigue; this in turn allows you to enjoy training for longer periods of time. Also you will be less likely to sustain injuries and bruising. Personally, I have no desire to spend my life walking round with black eyes, a fat lip and permanently bruised arms; it is neither healthy nor necessary, and certainly not big or clever.

If your opponent is strong and unyielding this need not be a problem, in fact it can be used to your advantage as their inflexibility can be manipulated to be the cause of their downfall. Over use of strength and heavy handedness will lead to stiff arms and over committed attacks. These are easily dealt with, because they are obvious in their intention; this creates in turn an obvious choice of counter attack. Also, if your opponent has tense arms this will enable you to gain control over their body; if you pull or push the arm, the body will move in a predictable (exploitable) way. Any habits, quirks, or predictable behaviour in Chi sau, can be seen as a weakness to be capitalised upon.

During Chi sau practice the mind must be focused and unclouded by everyday thought; herein lies a meditational similarity [see being in the moment]. The need to concentrate and be single minded clears the mind and stops us from thinking about anything else. Often training will reach the level of pure, subconscious reflex, where there is no time to think of anything at all. At this point we have to trust and rely on our body's automatic systems, switching off the conscious mind. Elite level athletes have always known of the need for a relaxed body and concentrated mind (a state often referred to as 'being in the zone').

Your brain can be seen as being divided into two halves. One half tends to plan things systematically and breaks strategies down into easy pieces. The other half tends to look at things in an intuitive, spatial way. When your body and mind are in tune with each other you will achieve your peak performance. A relaxed body and concentrated mind plays an important role in the efficient co-operation of these two systems.

Because Chi sau is all about learning sensitivity it is also quite easy to practise with one person blindfolded (I do not advise trying both!). This will heighten the sensitivity in the arms, as this is all they have to rely on. If you do practise blindfold, or with closed eyes, it is important to remember that the person with restricted vision, will be able to feel where your centre is, but may not be so aware of how close you are. So keep your head back!

Another interesting point about Chi sau is that it is impossible to tell how skilful a practitioner is by just watching. The only way you can judge another person is by training with them. By the same token training partners will feel different and distinct, even if the same teacher has taught them all. This is because of different body types, personalities, and different interpretations of technique. For this reason it is a good idea to train with as many different partners as possible, in this way you will gain experience of how to deal with a larger number of situations. However, when training with someone from a different school, it is always a good idea to lay down some ground rules (e.g. no full contact punches to the head). Ensure that you are both exploring each other's skill, and trading ideas, not necessarily trying to prove each other wrong, as this will usually degenerate from a useful training session, into a punch-up.

Chi Gerk

Chi gerk (sticky leg training) is necessary to train the legs so that they operate in a similar fashion to the hands.

Pic. 28. Chi Gerk training

That is to be responsive to forces, returning to a position of stability after defending against kicks, sweeps and trips. It also trains the practitioner to detect when it is appropriate for similar attacks to be launched from the legs.

Chi gerk is normally practised separately from Chi sau. Although it is possible to train both simultaneously, the range appropriate for legwork is somewhat closer, nearer grappling range, and tends to be more useful when normal positioning has broken down (Pic. 28). Chi gerk training is particularly handy if you wish to take control of an opponent, or take them to the ground, without punching or striking them.

Other useful concepts

Biu, Bik and Bong

Closely related to the hand changes and fundamental to the system are the concepts of Biu, Bik and Bong. Simply, these translate as forward, around and detain and could be seen as a further breakdown of the overall goal to occupy the centre line. To consolidate these nebulous ideas into a more solid equation we can see that:

Why Wing Chun Works

If a hand is free, or moves to a point beyond the area we need to defend, it takes the shortest path to the opponent's centre. If the hand meets any obstacles on the way, it must move efficiently around them and continue on the same, or on another path. Any attacks that invade our centre need to be intercepted and gently, but quickly absorbed, returned or deflected. If in doubt, stick.

It pays at this point to remember the famous Wing Chun saying that illustrates the system in a nut shell. Hand comes detain. Hand goes follow. Hand free thrust forward. It could be said that this simple little adage encapsulates the entire Wing Chun system.

Learning to not stop (flow)

At first glance Wing Chun seems to be composed of several different straight-line techniques (the shortest distance between two points). There are many short, sharp, percussive moves with frequent, rapid changes of direction and the ultimate aim is to knock down an opponent quickly, in order to stop them attacking you.

How then does this relate to the smooth, gentle, constantly flowing plan of Chi sau? Firstly there are just as many circles in Wing Chun as there are straight lines; in fact most of the linear movements originate in circular form. Consider the turn of the stance that transforms a straight-line attack into a straight-line return of force. Every time one of our attacks is blocked, jammed or deflected, a circle is employed to re-route it to centre.

We need to remain relaxed in order to allow us to change direction in mid stroke, without stopping to think about the next move. Without this smooth, seamless feel Wing Chun can become too staccato and changes in direction would involve stopping and re-planning. This spikiness would be detrimental to smooth efficient technique, intentions will be telegraphed to the opponent and if they are skilful they will dissolve any attack and slip through to your centre.

In the initial stages of learning a movement it is often necessary to break down the technique into easy pieces. Once the movement is absorbed we can string the stages back together again. In a similar way independent movements and position changes need to be strung together seamlessly.

You should end up with a constant, uninterrupted flow towards centre. An opponent can no more stem the flow of motion than they could stay dry if you threw a bucket of water over them. When practising rolling in Chi sau, the change in direction should be smooth and subtle. When we breathe there is a top and bottom to our breath but the change from inhalation to exhalation goes unnoticed, we are not aware of it unless we are gasping for breath. The roll in Chi sau should change direction in this same rounded, cyclic way.

When viewed from certain angles the hand shapes in Chi sau or Tai Chi pushing hands look remarkably similar to the ancient Yin Yang symbol, representing balance and equality through opposites. Tan sau and Bong sau, like Yin and Yang can be seen as opposite ideas; Yin in this case could be the soft or yielding hand, like that of Bong sau, leading a partner into over committing. The Yang could be the hand (or side) as it contains energy; Tan sau for instance, creating a strong yet mobile barrier. As one side, or hand changes over, so must the other. Two hands containing strength or two soft hands would be equally dangerous. Any movements (defence or attack) in Chi sau should be synchronised with the opponent's timing, in this way they will feel more natural and so be harder to detect and react to.

Solo Forms

In order to achieve smooth precision movements it is necessary to practice solo. This allows us to learn the ways in which our bodies can move and programs in the basic movement control patterns [see contact reflexes]. We also need to understand what effect these movements will have on our position and how we can change quickly and smoothly from one position to another. The effectiveness of Wing Chun is dependant on the clear understanding of several aspects of body mechanics:

1. **Correct and efficient use of muscle energy.**
2. **The accuracy and angle of joints (wrist, elbow, shoulders and back).**
3. **The movement of the upper body in relation to the lower body (alignment of hips and movement at waist).**
4. **Use of the stance whilst in motion (stepping and turning) and the effect this has on our hands.**

The six Wing Chun forms teach us all of the above progressing in an easy to learn and systematic way. They contain all of the concepts central to the system (apart from positioning and sensitivity to a partner learned in Chi sau) and many techniques.

There are 4 open hand forms, one performed against a specifically designed wooden dummy, and two weapon sets; the long pole and butterfly knives.

The forms contain all that is necessary to develop and maintain good body habits, working through the musculature and joint system, training them in a progressive manner. Any additions or alterations to the forms could alter, or detract from the overall system and for this reason they should be practised as they are. It is perfectly simple to test new theories by designing new exercises or drills.

For many people, forms or katas involve pretending to fight one or more imaginary opponents; this is not always true of Wing Chun. You cannot have a fight on your own and, as Wing Chun often concerns itself with concepts, as opposed to specific techniques, this method can restrict understanding of the system. It is often more useful to keep the interpretation of the forms conceptual and broad, than to tie every movement down with a specific, unchangeable purpose. From simple concepts spring a wealth of ideas and techniques. The same is not always true for the reverse.

The forms contain many of the principles central to the system; as you search through them your ideas may change and move on. This is OK; the forms have been designed in an abstract way to prevent students becoming trapped in them. Provided the essential rules are adhered to, you can do whatever you like. The forms are a path to freedom, not one of restriction.

Siu Lim Tao (see form posters in back of book)

The first form is called Siu Lim Tao, meaning little idea or small thought (to me it also means, think about the details, small movements matter or just keep it simple). This form is the seed from which the whole system will grow. As a tree that needs strong roots to hold it up, so the first form and all the concepts held within it must be fully understood in order for a student to progress successfully.

The form is split into three sections with a different emphasis on each, but the overall aim is to achieve a good stance and triangulation, with relaxed arms that can act independently from the trunk of the body. To this end many of the movements are performed on one arm at a time, whilst the other arm is kept isolated in the ready position. Siu Lim Tao contains reference points for all the basic techniques, so make sure you get it right from the outset.

The opening shows us how to find the correct stance, defines the centre line and demonstrates the centre punch. This is also the correct order of importance: Stance, centre, and attack.

The first section introduces the unbendable arm and trains us to develop the muscles and joints of the arm and wrist in the proper way, without involving excessive movement of the shoulders. The prying force of Tan sau, Fook sau and Wu sau are also introduced. This section should be performed slowly and deliberately, with all movement driven from the elbow. Some people liken the concentration to a meditative state; small thought is, after all, what is required for meditation. The section closes with Pac sau, a centre palm and the rolling wrist, which develops and stretches the muscles of the forearm.

The second section teaches the correct use of force in any direction. The arms should be relaxed until the final inches of each move where energy is released, producing the percussive impact characteristic of Wing Chun. After each release the arms should immediately return to their relaxed state and continue directly to the next position. Often both arms will perform the same move on opposing sides of the body. This has a balancing effect making excessive body movements less likely for the beginner. This section of the form should be performed briskly.

The third section, describing basic shapes, opens with Pac sau, side palm and rolling wrist, going on to demonstrate Tan sau applications with Gaun sau, Huen sau and low palm, Bong sau with Tan sau and Toc sau or heel palm, then finally, two arms working together to recover from a compromised position. This section should be practised with an emphasis on correct positions and use of elbow energy. The form closes with 3 punches and rolling wrist.

Chum Kiu (see form posters in back of book)

After having learned to isolate the arms from the body and understood the basic stance, the second form Chum Kiu (searching for, or crossing the bridge) teaches us how to move our bodies around an opponent or force, whilst maintaining the skills found in Siu Lim Tao. Again the form can be split into 3 sections, making it easier to understand, but the purpose of each section is not considered to be so specific. Generally the first section teaches turning on the spot, unfolding to the correct range, and Lap sau. Bong sau is considered to be in contact and on the outside line. The change from Bong to Lap sau with correct elbow positioning is also introduced.

The second section begins with a turn to 90 degrees with Lan sau, and introduces the lifting kick. Lan sau is kept low to prevent an opponent using it to push against. Lateral footwork is used for gaining contact or side stepping under pressure, the centre line is at 90 degrees to the direction in which you are stepping. Bong sau is considered to be out of, and trying to gain, contact. Bong sau can also be used on the inside line in this manner. The punch can be interpreted as an uppercut, but is generally seen as travelling straight to the target.

The third section shows us the front kick, forward footwork with the half step, step together (full step) which also gives us the option to change to any other direction, step back, T step and angled kick. Several methods of close body control are also demonstrated, such as Low Bong sau, pushing from the stance and Gum sau to cover the lower gates against kicks or low punches. Finally punching to cover an exposed gate is demonstrated. The overall theme of Chum Kiu is gaining contact with an opponent then, crossing over the bridge to their centre by virtue of correct positioning and angle.

Muk Yan Chong

Wooden dummy training forms an intrinsic part of the Wing Chun system. Literally translated Muk Yan Chong means, a stake used as a dummy. Other styles of Kung fu use dummies to practice against but the Wing Chun dummy and its form is specifically designed to practise and improve Wing Chun skills. The form has undergone many changes throughout its history; originally it consisted of 140 movements. The great Grandmaster Yip Man thought this number too numerous and reduced them to 108 (considered a lucky number by Chinese people). Later though he decided that some vital parts were missing and increased the amount to 116 techniques where it is generally accepted to remain to this day (although there are many different versions of this form).

Training in the wooden dummy form will improve many aspects of skill, especially your ability to move freely around an opponent, arriving in a strong position and hitting centre from a correct stance. Another useful effect of dummy training is that the pre-set angles of the arms will help to perfect the delivery of techniques and hone the angle of attack.

Why Wing Chun Works

It is of course possible to strike and kick the dummy with considerably more force than you could safely use against a partner. It must however be pointed out that the purpose of the wooden dummy is not to harden the arms or hands. The practitioner should not bash themselves recklessly into the arms, but aim to cling and stick to them until correct positioning allows a slip to the next position or strike. Lastly the dummy form contains many kicks, trips, traps and throws as well as combination movements not previously seen in the solo forms.

It is useful initially, to learn to perform repeated Kau sau techniques along with pivoting of the stance. The Gaun sau will be holding energy along the line of the arm, whilst the Kau sau will be just resting, the weight distribution will change as you apply upward pressure to the dummy arms, and the hip should push upwards to supply lift to the arm. As you pivot through, the Gaun sau relaxes and rolls over the top keeping contact with the arm (this is in fact Kau sau), whilst the other limb feels underneath its arm and energy is turned on as the weight is transferred to the opposite foot. The opposite Gaun sau position can now contain energy. When this technique can be performed with ease add the high palm off the low arm, or the low palm off the high arm combined with Fook sau, which pulls, from square, against the angle of the arm. High palm wedges inside against the arm, low palm drops clear of the arm it frees from. All sections in the form tie up in this way.

Section 1.

This section emphasises footwork and successful movement around the dummy, stress must be placed upon the practitioner's ability to arrive at the correct angle, with the hand shapes positioned comfortably and not cramped. In Bong and Tan sau the wrists should make smooth and gentle contact with the last couple of inches of the dummy arms. Remember where centre is as you travel. Do not be over concerned with striking the trunk at first; rather pay attention to your positioning and angle.

Section 2.

Repeat section 1. Starting on the other side.

Section 3.

Pak sau is demonstrated here, first on the inside gate with caution not to commit the whole arm and to spring back to centre each time. Then on the outside line, Pak on a pivot, or Jut sau. The movement is bounced into a chop and back to a safe trap and low strike. Low bong then leads into an unusual side angled attack or Man sau after the hand is freed with Pak sau followed by the counter attacking side kick. This kick is also useful if you are pursued down the flank, or if an over-committed Bong sau is pressed or trapped. Ensure that the force from the kick goes into the centre and that the foot does not slip off or down the trunk.

Section 4.

Learning to circle around a guard, making use of an opponent's strength to spring off and deliver a double-handed shock force. Pay attention to the bounce of the dummy and try to make good use of its rhythm. Bear in mind that double handed moves can also be performed by one hand. Then roll off Bong sau to Tan and low palm, the kick is delivered at 90 degrees to the leg.

Section 5.

This section deals mainly with Po Pai Chung or double palm strikes and pushes. Attention must be paid to the position of the opponent's guard. Your strike will be wedging from the inside or outside to trap or jam your opponent, or sometimes freeing your own hand in order to hit.

Section 6.

Bong sau pivoting into grappling hand is stressed here and this must be performed from a deep turn as opposed to a step. The grapple is combined with a chop to the throat, and doubled up with a centre palm from the inside gate. Also illustrated here is the cross step stamp kick where the kick is launched off the 'wrong' leg. This is often a kick to the opponent's rear, supporting leg. The cross step can also be used for a smooth direction change.

Section 7.

Kicking and throwing are shown in this section. First a front spade kick to the hip, groin or central area is delivered, this is then turned into a knee stomp kick in order to bring your weight back down to ground. Pay attention to the subtle footwork shift necessary to position yourself for the initial kick.

The throw is performed after Gum sau, a circle step slips in behind the lead leg of the opponent. The heel is raised and as contact is made on the calf muscle. Pak sau, Palm strike and heel stamp are performed virtually simultaneously causing the leg to be trapped and the opponent to be thrown backwards. This is similar to the skills gained in Chi gerk (sticky legs). Particular care and attention must be paid to centre, posture, timing and angle as you move through this technique if it is to be successful. Care must also be taken with the footwork as you move out to the other side.

Section 8.

The final section concludes the form with a kick delivered from a low, then high parry, on a slightly longer range than most. This is then followed with Bong sau into grappling Lap sau performed with both hands, on the turn, whilst the foot is swept/stamped forwards and down onto the opponent's ankle or foot. This will jam the leg against the direction of the pull causing them to trip and be thrown forwards.

Biu Tze

Biu Tze (flying fingers) is the mysterious third form of Wing Chun. The mystery surrounding it stems from the fact that it is often only taught to loyal students who have shown themselves to be capable of a high level of development, both through the system and on a personal level.

Frequently it is only taught on a one to one basis and a student must certainly have absorbed all the concepts from Siu Lim Tao and Chum Kiu, frequently the dummy form is also considered to apply before Biu Tze. The emphasis on energy is put in the elbows, fingertips and hand. Many of the moves come up from under the bridge and often from the 'wrong side' of the body.

The form can be interpreted as an attacking form and certainly contains many sophisticated ideas. It can however also be

Why Wing Chun Works

seen as supplying methods for cutting back to the centre after an over-commitment, or as an escape when leverage or centre is lost. For this reason Biu Tze is also sometimes known as the emergency form. This is another reason for the form not to be shown too early in a person's training, it is better to learn not to make mistakes, than to find ways of correcting them after they have been made. Often, when an artist is learning to sketch, the teacher will not allow them to use an eraser, in this way the student has to live with their mistakes and so learns not to repeat them.

Weapon Sets

Luk Dim Boon Quan

Luk Dim Boon Quan, literally translates as six and a half point long pole. The Wing Chun pole form is believed to have been introduced around the time of the Red Junk opera troop. It is a short form and introduces the basic parries and attacks; there are only six and a half techniques, hence the name. Practicing the pole form will help develop strength in the wrists and stance.

Sticky Poles

It is possible to practice sticky pole techniques with a partner; the idea is to stick to the end of the partners' pole maintaining a strong position and good range. This skill is not unlike fencing. When an opening becomes available trap the pole, strike through or slide down the other pole to attack the hands.

Sticky pole practise exaggerates footwork manoeuvres and positioning, so it is very useful as a training method. It is also possible to train with a pole against butterfly knives.

Bart Cham Dao

Bart Cham Dao (Eight broadsword cutting techniques) clearly dates to a time when kung fu skills were a matter of life and death. Despite popular belief, open hand fighting would be practically useless against a skilled, armed warrior.

The Bart Cham Dao is also known as the butterfly knives form because of the appearance of the blades when crossed.

Why Wing Chun Works

The form is in eight sections demonstrating the various defensive and attacking manoeuvres.

The knives are used as an extension of the hand shapes and many of the common techniques can be performed with knives. When fighting the aim is to attack the opponents weapon arms first. The blades are often one sided to allow them to be rotated back along the forearm for close range operation. The thumb or tine on the guard can be used to trap a weapon but is also used to rotate the blade so this must be smooth, rounded and accessible to the thumb of the holding hand.

In the present day practice with swords and pole could be seen as obsolete, however the form is very useful, supplying a different type of footwork and positioning. The weight and balance of the blades is also a very effective way of training for posture and wrist strength.

Wing Chun for Life

Health or Fitness?

On an aerobic fitness level, an energetic session of Wing Chun can certainly get your cardiovascular system working harder, but I personally believe it affects overall health, with fitness as a secondary benefit. High levels of aerobic fitness can be achieved by playing any sport, although the highly competitive nature of these games will not appeal to everyone.

Solo exercise is also an option, with activities such as circuit training, step aerobics or jogging, but whilst these activities and others like them increase your strength and fitness, there is no real refinement of skill involved because there is little learning taking place. Once you have learned the basics you are not doing anything new, there is no precision to improve upon, only strength or endurance. This lack of intellectual challenge could be seen as less satisfying to the individual, so there could be less motivation and reason to continue (other that pre-paid gym membership). Training in Wing Chun can involve a lifetimes honing of technique, position and sensitivity.

Why Wing Chun Works

If your health was a car

There seems to be a fundamental difference between the Eastern and Western ideals of health. The Western ideal seems to be to bolt-on bigger carburettors, power exhausts systems, larger wheels and go faster stripes.

The Eastern ideal is perhaps more of a holistic approach, oil and lubricate all the relevant places, service the vehicle regularly, replace the filters, keep the cooling system clear and don't over stress the engine.

The emphasis is on care rather than repair. Prevention is better than cure and regular practice of Wing Chun will help loosen the joints, condition and tone virtually all the musculature and help improve posture.

Pic.29.

Modern lifestyles require our minds to constantly take in vast amounts of information; our heads are normally so crammed with thoughts, ideas and plans that there is no space left for relaxation. Like a computer with too many applications opened our minds slow down and our bodies rebel (this is what we call stress).

The relaxed but focused nature of Wing Chun enables us to become more familiar with ourselves, and the way our bodies (as well as those of other people) work in conjunction with our minds. Chi sau allows us to concentrate, and yet switch our heads off for a while and let the body have a go in the driving seat.

This training can help reduce and put into perspective everyday stress and anxiety. Fitness of the mind and body has been proven to be beneficial to good health. Practitioners of Yoga, Tai Chi and Qigong (Chi Gung) will be familiar with this holistic concept of concentrating completely on exercise (or position, or balance) as a method of improving the body's natural defence mechanisms.

Spirituality

Many attempts have been made to attach religious or philosophical meaning to the physical practice of Kung Fu. However, spirituality need not mean religion, anybody who is deeply involved in any art form will find some kind of spirituality through it. This is as true for martial arts as it is for music, painting or poetry. By immersing ourselves in our art we can express outwardly something of our innermost self. Through this process we learn more about who we are and what we want; we hope that this is of benefit to ourselves and perhaps also, a guide to others.

Being in the Moment

Chi sau is a perfect physical demonstration of the concept of 'being in the moment'. The nature of Chi sau negates the importance of conscious thought; there are no plans or sequences that can be applied since Chi sau, like the moment is in a constant state of flux. As soon as you try to explain or define the moment it has passed. Any definition of a moment is a historical statement, since it describes what was and not what is. In the same way, if you tell someone, the time is exactly five o'clock, you will never be accurate because by the time you finish saying it, that time will have passed.

Living in the moment is extremely difficult since we have both a memory of previous moments and a sense of anticipation about the future ones. Trying to concentrate on the moment as it happens is hard. Your mind is a turmoil of disorganised thoughts, fears, conceptions, memories, etc. In daily life all of these things contribute to the way we live our lives.

If we had no memories we would not have personalities, neither would we be able to remember where we put the toothpaste! If we had no fear it would only be a matter of time before we were run over by a car, and without conceptions it would be impossible for us to make sense of the complexities of the world in which we live.

Chi sau puts the whole thing on a simple physical level. This can help us put things into perspective. Our interpretation of Chi sau can be limited (with the aid of a blindfold, or closed eyes) to only one of our five senses, touch! Sensitivity to force makes Chi sau an excellent vehicle for achieving a sense of unity with the moment since it has a purity of perception not found in the other senses.

We can see or hear something approaching before it arrives; this allows time for the conscious mind to form conceptual notions about whatever it is we are about to encounter (anticipation). Herein lies the error in interpretation since we have now added something of ourselves to the situation so purity of response is impossible.

With touch however, only the moment matters. We can only feel something when it is in contact with us, not a fraction before or a fraction after. There is no room for misinterpretation; a force is exactly as heavy as it is, no more and no less.

To be able to respond instantaneously to forces in Chi sau requires us to rely on touch and disengage the conceptual part of our minds from the activity. Planning or the desire to do something specific have no place in Chi sau since it is the ever changing nature of the forces that we must respond to, not our own whims, desires and fears. Do not try to make things happen; learn to live in the moment as it happens around you, learn to trust the built in reflexes and they will automatically place you in the openings as they occur.

Do not try to grasp at opportunities that you have missed, they are already gone. There is nothing to seize in the constant motion of life, you can no more seize an opportunity than you can seize the wind. Try to seize the wind and the best you will get is stale air. Stand in the wind let it blow past you and through you, live each moment of it. Enjoy the wind for its strength and speed at one moment and for its softness and stillness at another. It exists and you exist, it blows and you feel it blow, nothing more nothing less.

If you run for the bus but it leaves without you, your intention was to catch it but you didn't. You can look back and say, If only I had left earlier, if only I had run faster. But you didn't; you left when you left and you ran as fast as you ran, these things are now passed moments and regret will not alter them, the situation is now and you must live in the moment of waiting for the next bus; being unable to wait for the next bus leaves you lost in time just as much as being unable to step on the bus as it arrives. Doing and not doing are the same, they are response to circumstance. If you learn to appreciate the moment and live in it, your responses will be appropriate, what more can we ask of ourselves?

When practising Chi sau, let your head learn from your limbs, not the other way around. Your arms, if left to themselves, are pure and devoid of thought, all they have is the sensitivity to change and the programmed reflexes.

If we can switch off the constant babble in our heads just for a while and allow our arms to do what they need, we will tap into a vital resource. This space that we gain for ourselves here is free of desire, fear, anticipation, self consciousness and all the other things that clutter up the mind and make our responses to everyday situations clumsy or inappropriate, based as they are on an attitude that tries to take into account both the past and the future. An attitude that tries to inject our egos into everything, and tries desperately to grasp onto pieces of life whilst flinging other pieces away.

Modelling Problem Solving

Training to redirect physical forces can enable you to reduce the inevitable emotional or psychological conflict, which we are all bound to encounter in life.

By training our bodies to deal with external physical force our minds become better equipped to understand the nature of the moment. The solutions to problems seem easier to find, and we become better equipped to deal with every day stress and strain.

All of us have to contend with mental, emotional or physical violence at some point in our lives. Human movement, constrained as it is by physical limitations, is easier to understand and translate. This understanding can lead us to a set of guidelines based around the Wing Chun concepts.

Used correctly these principles can be applied on all levels, so enabling us to deal with conflict on an emotional level, not meeting it head on, nor running away, but rather by adopting a mental attitude that allows us to understand and reduce the discord as it happens; neither anticipating nor regretting the consequences. Remaining flexible, changing and adapting to circumstances, translating problems in order to control them. Using these concepts a potentially harmful situation can be disarmed, an emotional problem can be solved and everyday mental stress and strain can be put into proper perspective and reduced in a calm, and effective manner.

As we know it is necessary for the body to act, physically, like a rotating cylinder. Any force applied to its circumference will cause it to rotate in the same direction as the force. As one side moves back, the other side moves forward, rotating around the centre. In this way it is possible to dispel and return a force. Think of this, not as trying to avoid and hit our opponent but as becoming a vehicle to transport our opponent's energy and return it from whence it came. The result is not our fault, the aggressor made it happen.

So now let us look at this process from a philosophical standpoint, it is possible to apply these concepts to life and to the every day problems we inevitably find there.

To solve a problem we need to be able to ascertain exactly what the problem is from an unbiased viewpoint. We need to understand what our position is relative to the problem, and how it relates to us. We then need to work out what are our options and what effect they will have on the whole situation. Finally, when we make a decision, we must be direct and positive in our attitude, yet flexible enough to change our angle of approach as circumstances dictate or as new problems arise. We need to move forward to meet the problem, not head on but in a way that enables us to take in the whole picture. This enables us to see the most suitable way to approach it. If you are unable to succeed from one angle, look at it from another perspective, try to feel another way in.

Often an argument is won by applying enough pressure to force an adversary into over-committing themselves, or admitting something in the heat of the moment that they would have preferred to keep to themselves (watch a lawyer in court!). This is true in many situations. If two people are arguing, it is often the one with a cool head who gains the upper hand because they do not make rash statements without considering the consequences.

Pic.30.

Not being over-committed also gives you more chance to recover should you be caught wrong-footed. If you are firmly committed to a single standpoint, the moment someone finds a chink in your armour you are on shaky ground.

Each and every one of the concepts that we apply physically can be translated, in a similar fashion, into methods for dealing with the problems and inflexible attitudes that every day life constantly throws at us. Whether it is a matter of achieving an objective, or dealing with a situation at work or home that has been thrust upon us, a method can be found to ease the pressure. Stress, like tension, comes from within. So we need to train for an efficient and sensitive mind, as well as body, to deal with the problems life sets for us.

Defining and using a centre line, makes everything else we do more simple to understand, and so more simple to achieve. It enables us to break a situation down into bite size, manageable units and allows us to predict defensive requirements depending on angle. In the same way if we can fit a framework around a problem it will help us see it objectively in order to model it accurately. The concept of centre can help us find a focused and direct route to the solution of a dichotomy, whilst being able to maintain a well-balanced opinion of two possible solutions.

The principles of triangulation, coupled with an astute awareness of range and of our own position relative to that of the problem, will allow us to approach a situation from a position of strength. This gives us space to manoeuvre and change, without getting trapped, or entangled.

In the same way, if we allow a problem to get on top of us, we can become embroiled in it, finding it hard to disentangle fact from our own exaggerations and paranoia. This will make the problem seem impossible to solve. If on the other hand we can hold the situation away from us, (but not let it get out of reach -we need to solve it, not pretend it isn't there) we can see it in proper perspective. There is always a way to cope, no matter how serious or awful the trouble may at first seem.

Touch sensitivity and contact reflexes play the part of communication and trigger, sending out valuable information and warning us of pitfalls and danger when vision, thought and action are not quick enough. By waiting for information to come to us by way of feel and touch, we are less likely to be sold a dummy, and the reflex is instantaneous. So rather than charging in feet first or just trying to beat somebody to the punch, we can condition ourselves to instinctively 'know' what is coming. We can then deal with it using the appropriate technique. These ideas are akin to those well-known qualities we, all too often, could do with a little more of. Patience, perception and communication skills.

Bide your time until conditions are ready, before proceeding with your plan of action. Wait to see which way a situation will swing before you decide what to say or do, but above all listen to the people around you and talk to them to gain feed back about ideas and plans. Do not be insensitive! In practice, if you are pushed off centre, you should not use force to try and realign. If you struggle with someone who is stronger, or in a more powerful position, you may well come off worst.

Use your sensitivity to slip around and cut back to your aim, from a different angle. Clearly, this goes hand in hand with having a flexible, resilient and adaptable attitude, and not committing yourself past the point of no return. If you meet an obstruction or interruption, you need to find another way around the problem, rather than banging your head on it.

Some people feel that, at some point in their lives, they have missed out on a golden opportunity. This may have been through doubt or hesitancy, saying afterwards: If only I had done it when I had the chance. Or: Why didn't I think of that before?

Often the people who take opportunities and turn them to their immediate or long-term advantage, are called lucky and are told that they always land on their feet. This is not true; these lucky people usually have a way of turning a situation to their advantage. Their minds seem to be naturally inclined to feel out, find, and seize opportunity as it flashes past. They are not always successful, but often seem to be so, to the more pedestrian amongst us.

Biu, Bik and Bong, the Wing Chun Model.

- Biu - forward, direct, through.
- Bik - around, above, under, about.
- Bong - detain, receive, hold onto, absorb, deflect.

If there are no obstructions we move forward, if we meet a problem we go around it (solving it using our sensitivity). If something causes a threat to us we deflect or detain it, in order to understand more fully how to deal with it.

Now, this is all very conceptual, pure theory. No specific examples have been given as the possibilities are endless. Clearly it will not be quite this simple in practice. It is no mean feat to defend oneself from physical assault. In the same way, it can be difficult to remain calm and cool when someone, whom you know to be wrong, is having a heated argument with you, and won't listen to your point of view.

There is no easy way to follow these ideas, just as there is no quick way to learn the physical exercises. Competence springs from practice and confidence springs from knowing what you are capable of doing.

Using your comprehension of the system, trial and error, and your ability to turn to use what is available, you must work to discover that elusive quality that binds together all the related principles and makes the transition from theory, to practical ability, and back again to a philosophy that can help you live life with less struggle.

Why Wing Chun Works

As a final word I would mention that in class I teach only physical movement. Attaching any kind of doctrinal message to Wing Chun would spoil its inherent simplicity, and limit its audience as a very practical martial art. Whilst it can be interesting, and indeed useful, to intellectualise beyond the physical, this in truth, is not what Wing Chun is.

Contact Us

The Wing Chun Federation was founded by Alan Gibson (Black sash fourth degree) in 1990. The Federation's objective is to teach Wing Chun Kung Fu in a relaxed and accessible manner, where emphasis is placed on good technique and personal development rather than violence and aggression. Wing Chun can be simply learnt by commitment and patience. Age, sex or physical size is of no consequence, and a high level of proficiency can be obtained quickly and with ease. We are a non political organisation.

The Wing Chun Federation also runs regular self defence for women courses, where the student will learn the essentials of defending themselves against would be attackers, as well as how to avoid dangerous or uncomfortable confrontations where possible.

Representatives can be found in Southampton, Winchester, Salisbury, Romsey, Crowthorne, Isle of Wight, and Bournemouth.

Why Wing Chun Works

To contact the Wing Chun Federation about lessons and seminars, please write to:

Alan Gibson
The Wing Chun Federation,
12 Park Rd
Chandlers Ford
Eastleigh
Hants
SO53 2EU
U.K.

Pager: 07654 220170(4)

e mail: alan@wingchun.org.uk

Or visit our web site at:
http://www.wingchun.org.uk

Practising Siu Lim Tao regularly is the best way to train the body and mind for good Wing Chun.

Opening the form, find the stance and keep it.

003 Bend the knees

004 Push toes out

005 Push heels out to find basic stance

006 Cross arms to define centre line

007 lift up and out

008 Withdraw fists

009 Left fist in centre

010 Left punch

011 - 014 Huen sau (conditioning stretch)

015 Clench fist

016 Pull fist back briskly

017 - 020 Repeat punch and stretch on right side.

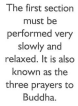

The first section must be performed very slowly and relaxed. It is also known as the three prayers to Buddha.

021 - 022 The prying force of Tan sau is introduced, perpendicular to the body and pushed out by the elbow.

023 - 024 Huen sau

025 - 027 Wu sau, keep the wrist on centre line and draw elbow to side of body.

028 - 029 Fook sau, keep the wrist on centre line and press elbow forward.

030 - 031 Huen sau.

032 - 045 Repeat Fook sau, Huen sau and Wu sau two more times, slowly.

   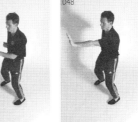 

046 Left Pac sau.

047 Hand returns to centre line.

048 Push out a straight lifting palm.

049 Huen sau stretch

050 Pull fist back swiftly

051 - 068 Repeat section on right side.

Second section, performed briskly with the arms relaxed until the last inches of each move.

069 Left gum sau.

070 Right Gum sau

071 Pull hands up together, behind body.

072 Push palm heels down behind body.

073 Pull up to waist level.

155

074 Bring hands to front.

075 Press palm heels down in front of body.

076 Raise elbows to Lan sau position, lower than shoulders.

077 - 078 Fak sau, drop elbows back first to allow edge of hands to travel in a straight line.

079 Return to Lan sau position.

080 - 081 Sink elbows and move to Gong sau, fingertips level with shoulders.

082 Rotate forearms.

083 Jut sau, jerk down and back from elbows.

Third section, basic techniques performed briskly and relaxed with energy at the end of the moves.

084 Biu sau, fingers relaxed.

085 Straight arms press down (hand goes straight to target).

086 Straight arms press up (hand goes straight to target).

087 Form fists and pull both back briskly.

088 Left Pak sau.

089 Wrist moves back to left side.

090 Left Side Palm strike.

091 - 092 Huen sau stretch and pull back fist.

093 - 096 Repeat Pak, Strike, Huen and pull back on right side.

097 Left hand drops to waist level.

156

098 Blocking Tan sau.

099 - 100 Whisk arm down to Gaun sau, the elbow moves to the hip.

101 Return directly to Tan sau.

102 Huen sau.

103 Low palm strike.

104 Huen sau stretch.

105 Pull fist back swiftly.

106 - 113 Repeat Tan, Gaun, Tan, Huen, etc. on right side.

114 Bong sau, wrist on centre, elbow lower than the shoulder.

115 Rotate to Tan sau.

116 Palm strike / Tok sau.

117 Huen sau stretch.

118 Pull fist back.

119 - 123 Repeat Bong, Tan, strike etc. on right.

157

124 Left wrist presses down centre.

125 Right hand by left elbow.

126 - 127 Replace left arm with right, withdraw left from elbow.

128 - 130 Repeat two more times, ending with left fist on centre line.

131 - 133 Left punch, right punch, left punch. Withdraw right fist, left Huen sau stretch.

134 Withdraw left fist.

135 close stance and push both hands down to sides.

158

Simple Thinking: Intelligent Fighters
(Why Wing Chun Works 2)

In the exiting sequel to his very popular first book 'Why Wing Chun Works', Alan Gibson explains how individual techniques and positions evolve as a result of the underlying Wing Chun concepts, and the forces we are likely to meet in combat.
Detailed photography, and clearly explained text, describe how fighting applications relate to Wing Chun theory. This book will undoubtedly become an invaluable reference work, both for Wing Chun practitioners and to all other thinking martial artists. The book also has Chum Kiu, (Wing Chun's second form) completely demonstrated in numbered photographs.

Simple Thinking: Intelligent Fighters (Why Wing Chun Works 2) £12.00
All prices include postage and packaging.
Send a cheque / postal order made out for **Alan Gibson** and include your address.
Send to:
The Wing Chun Federation
12 Park Rd
Chandlers Ford
Eastleigh
SO53 2EU

Only available in the U.K. Please allow 28 days for delivery.

The Wing Chun Forms: Combat Textbooks (Why Wing Chun Works 3)

by Alan Gibson

Be taken us on a detailed journey through the first two empty-hand forms and the unique Wooden Dummy form. Together, these three forms constitute the basic training methods and combat philosophy of the Wing Chun system. After finishing this book, the reader will have a detailed knowledge of the depth of the information contained within the forms, and have been inspired to discover greater insights into the Wing Chun personal combat system. A superb reference, this book is a must for every martial arts library. Wooden Dummy Form fully illustrated in back pages.

The Wing Chun Forms: Combat Textbooks (Why Wing Chun Works 3) £11.95
All prices include postage and packaging.
Send a cheque / postal order made out for Alan Gibson, state which poster you require and include your address.
Send to:
The Wing Chun Federation
12 Park Rd
Chandlersford
Eastleigh
SO53 2EU

Only available in the U.K. Please allow 28 days for delivery.